salve

words for the journey

ALSO BY PAGER PUBLICATIONS, INC.

—

in-Training: Stories from Tomorrow's Physicians

Family Doc Diary: A Resident Physician's Reflections in Fifty-Two Entries

in-Training: Stories from Tomorrow's Physicians, Volume 2

salve

words for the journey

MONISHA VASA, MD

PAGER PUBLICATIONS, INC.
a 501c3 non-profit literary corporation

Salve: Words For The Journey

Published by Pager Publications, Inc. at pagerpublications.org.

Printed in the United States of America.

Cover photograph and design by Ajay Major.
Book design by Ajay Major.

Volume 1
First Printing: 2019

ISBN-10: 0-578-57240-0
ISBN-13: 978-0-578-57240-6

Fierce love,
for you
whose light has been dimmed
in an already dark world—

For you
whose voice has been muted
in a loud screaming world—

For you
who feels lost
in a world full of mirrors—
Breathe.

When every warm body
is out of reach,
you have the power
to hold your own heart
like no other.

You can look up
and see yourself in the
moon and stars
and know that you
are never alone.

Hold on,
with me, for me,
for the light,
for your voice,
for the next step,
to guide you home.

contents

pager publications, inc.

Salve: Words For The Journey
is sponsored by Pager Publications, Inc.

Pager Publications, Inc. is a 501c3 nonprofit literary organization
that curates and supports peer-edited publications
for the medical education community.

The organization strives to provide students and educators
with dedicated spaces for the free expression of their distinctive voices.

Pager Publications, Inc. was officially incorporated in January 2015
by its founders Ajay Major, Aleena Paul and Erica Fugger
to provide administrative and financial support for
this book and other print and online publications.

foreword

CAYCE HOWE

I was raised a blue collar kid who somehow, as a teenager, fell in love with the idea of enlightenment. My search for this mysterious freedom in the late 80's led me to the used books left to me by the hippies of my parents' generation. These gems were laid out in the open on the shelves of Berkeley's cool bookstores, like Moes, Black Oak, and Shakespeare & Co. I would seek out wisdom in the dustiest of pages—the more obscure, the better.

In my seeking, I was open to whatever came my way. I was not bound by a religion or dogma that would confine me to a particular set of teaching. I did have one rule however, a rule that I steadfastly abided by: I would only read books by true practitioners. Only experiencers of the truth, not those merely regurgitating their own version of it. I would seek out the Yogis, the Shamans, the Tibetan Rinpoches, the beings who relied on the long arduous task of self-reflection as their source for wisdom.

That meant no scholars, no academics.

You see, back then, in my blunt naïveté, I didn't have any role models like Dr. Monisha Vasa. I didn't know of anyone who could transcend a title enough to be what the title represented. When I first met Monisha, I thought I was meeting a psychiatrist. Now I see her clearly as the medicine woman, healer, and wisdom holder that she is. A woman who has been in the trenches. A woman who has bent down to lift others up so many times that she jumped down there with them. A woman who is unafraid to show you the scars of such undertakings, the vulnerability and the fierce strength that comes along the way.

What you hold in your hands are words ground from the mortar and pestle of experience. When a person has held hands with others in the depths of suffering, and guided them to safety often enough for long enough, she starts to figure out the routes. These poems mark the way-points.

Of course, these wisdom words are not just for the heavy suffering. They are for anyone who wishes to align back into wholeness. That part of all of us that can weather the storm of life without becoming it.

I wish the younger part of me had broken my rule way back then. I wish this book had existed then, and that I would have flipped through the pages. It would have changed my mind about academic types. But more importantly, it would have furthered my journey. I would have set it on my bookshelf next to the other books written by mystics I held in such high regard. In fact, that's where it's sitting right now.

Cayce Howe
Senior Meditation Teacher, InsightLA
Authorized Teacher in The Theravada Buddhist Lineage

from the publisher

ALEENA PAUL, MD, MBA

I found the words of *Salve* to be a great comfort as I stood at a cross-roads, reflecting on the type of physician I wanted to be, on what I wanted to accomplish in my life, and on the journey that brought me through the many years of medical school and residency training.

With each piece I read, I remembered and relived moments with my patients, nights with my family, and visits with friends. I remembered the healthy, the sick, the ones who recovered, and the ones who did not.

Whether you are patient or physician, parent or child, lost or found, the words of *Salve* will guide you on your journey.

When we founded Pager Publications, Inc. in 2014, we strove to find and amplify voices that make the world of medicine a richer experience for patients and clinicians alike. We sought to highlight the stories of everyday people doing ordinary work that brings comfort and healing to the sick. We endeavor to return to the core of what medicine is—forging connections, building trust, and understanding the personal narratives of illness and health.

Salve: Words For The Journey, this magnificent opus by Dr. Monisha Vasa, is an exemplar of the paradigm-shifting work that we seek to promote, and our team at Pager Publications, Inc. is honored to publish this book.

Dr. Vasa's poetry is deeply introspective and asks you, her reader, to pause, to take a breath, and to truly notice yourself and the world around you. Through her work, Dr. Vasa embodies the ideals of a humanistic physician, one who listens without judgement and cares with compassion. Her writings bring her thoughtfulness and spirit directly into your hands. She guides, she encourages, she teaches.

I know that I will be turning to *Salve* many times in the future when I need direction and reflection. I invite you all to do the same.

Aleena Paul, MD, MBA
Founder and Treasurer of Pager Publications, Inc.

preface

MONISHA VASA, MD

*Barn's burnt down
now I can see the moon.*

Mizuta Masahide

This book that you hold in your hands is an invitation borne of many years of sitting with my patients. Day by day, hour by hour, I've been listening, learning and changing in response to what I've witnessed along the way. This journey through life brings us right up against joy, fear, heartbreak, love, loneliness, pain, anger, and shame. Being a psychiatrist (and a human being) has taught me that having someone by our side— someone who asks us questions, provides solace and support, and mirrors ourselves back with wholehearted compassion—helps make the path bearable. Beautiful, even.

Yet there were only so many people who would ever walk through the doors of my office, and only so many hours I could sit with others. What about all the other hours of the day? What about all we feel in the hollows of night? How do we find the words we need when no one is around to witness our hardest moments?

Salve: Words For The Journey is that offering from me to you. It is an invitation to take these words wherever you go, so they are there for you when you need them. I do not want this book to remain in pristine condition or be displayed on a beautiful bookshelf. No. I want this book to be in your hands or bag or briefcase or purse or on the passenger seat. I want the cover torn and corners folded and paragraphs underlined and words highlighted and questions in the margins.

This is an invitation to use this book up, like life itself.

Let your heart guide how you read the pages ahead. Cover to cover. Back to front. Week by week. Poems and prompts. Your own writing next to mine. Open to a random page and discover a message or question meant for you.

There is no right way, only your way, to be with these words.

In this moment, I am grateful for the ability to express myself. To sit in a home, with a sense of safety and health around me, and write. I have a body and brain that work, most of the time. I have food in the fridge. I have children who are healthy. I have financial security that comes to me as a result of doing work I love. I don't acutely fear for my safety.

In my here and now, I can live in this space because I stand on the shoulders of my parents, who immigrated to this country and worked hard to provide for my education. I recognize that this is a reflection of my deep privilege.

When I close my eyes and feel a sense of gratitude in my heart for the gift of self-expression, I am also reminded of the tremendous responsibility that comes with it: to tell the truth, never to take for granted or abuse the power that comes with having a voice, and to do my best to use that power for good.

The final part of my invitation to you? I hope you share the words of your journey too, somewhere, with someone, in the ways that feel right. We want to hear your voice, because everything about what you say matters. May these pages be a gift and a blessing to you as you live your story.

Monisha Vasa, MD
Author of *Salve: Words For The Journey*

acknowledgments

How does a writer become a writer? It seems a writer is borne of a million small moments, a million microscopic interactions that, with a bit of magic and faith, result in words on the page. It is hard to acknowledge only a select few, so I will broadly say—thank you. Thank you to every person who has ever believed in my words, read them, or shared them. I am grateful, more than you know.

In particular, thank you to:

My parents, sister, and in-laws: for giving me shoulders to stand upon.

Dhiraj, Lakshmi, Rohan: for infinite love, and the daily space, time, and encouragement to write.

My psychiatry mentors and colleagues: for the training and support needed to dedicate my life to caring for those struggling with psychiatric illness.

Cayce Howe: for sharing the wisdom of mindfulness and meditation.

Jena Schwartz: for inspiring me to write my first poem, for reminding me to start and keep going, and for her brilliant coaching and editing.

Pager Publications, Inc.: for seeing something in my words, and for their mission to support physician writers.

My patients: for the honor of walking alongside you.

My friends (you know who you are): for just always being there, no matter what.

When I struggle to call myself a writer, I keep writing anyway because of what I see reflected in all of your eyes. May you always know what a gift each and every one of you has been to me, and may I return that back to you in spades. This book belongs to all of us, and I wouldn't have it any other way.

With love and blessings, Monisha

salve

For it is our cracks,
the eroding edges of our soul,
that keep us needing the salve of each other's touch.

potential

Before the poem,
floating words
visited me in the night.

Before the words,
breathing in the dark,
while I invited the words
to stay awhile
and warm the still air.

Before the breath,
a pause,
a space of noticing
the way my bones ached,
how my heart whispered.

And before the noticing,
there was a moment,
of beautiful nothing,
where potential bloomed
into words on paper,
and I came to life.

discover

Come with me,
and together,
let's discover
the velvet space
beneath our thoughts.

May we find there
a place to rest
a pause to breathe
a moment of peace
for the weary mind.

May we return
in the silence
to our infinite
and ever present
truth, and know
ourselves again.

listen

Sometimes,
we receive a message
from the heart:

something little
or something big
needs to change.

We must lean in close,
ear to the chest,
and listen.

Listen.

We will know the answer
when we hear it.

Poetry sent from the universe
in the sound of a voice.

Your own voice.

catch

Silence and nature will catch you every time you fall.

What catches you?

wisdom

Words visited me
in the call of the birds
and the rush of the wind
and in footsteps imprinted
ahead and behind of me.

All whispering a wisdom song
I often forget:

There is a time to run
and a time to rest.
We must find the quiet
to hear what our bones
are longing for.

No pride or shame in
chasing our dreams
with arms wide open,
or stopping to release
what doesn't belong
to us anymore.

The ground and sky
remind me:

No need to worry.

burden

Set your burden down, my friend.

Absence, loneliness, silence, grief
carry unspeakable weight.

Set your burden down, my friend.

Let the spaces fill
with the kaleidoscope color
of all that feels
real and true
for you.

Set your burden down, my friend.

All that is missing
rests deep within.

bittersweet

And somehow
time keeps moving,
we keep walking
tight-fisted,
only to remember
there is no grasping.

There is only letting go,
open-handed,
of everything other than
this bittersweet moment
with its soft spaces for
our words to land
between us.

barriers

The residue of yesterday
falls like ash
through our fingers.

The dreams of tomorrow
remain blank space.

All past and future,
should-haves and what-ifs,
spinning thoughts that
fill us with noise
masked as truth.

Remove the barriers
and step into now.

Clear.
Quiet.
Still.

Waiting to hold us
while we hold on
to everything else.

hope

Hope is a funny thing, isn't it?

Sometimes hope is the only thing that propels us forward, that keeps us holding on for a better tomorrow. But hope in some ways is a form of living in the future, outside of the truth of right now. Radical acceptance means embracing what is, as difficult as that may be.

When we relax fully into what is offered to us right now, we may discover an ease and spaciousness that we didn't previously feel. Perhaps our next step becomes slightly more clear, and we are led towards right action. Indeed, this is a moment by moment practice for me—this push and pull between full surrender and desire for change.

What happens when we surrender our resistance to what is?

longing

You recognize longing
in the way her breath
catches in her chest.

And you must ask,
What is it, dear one?
What is the name
of all you ache for?

On your knees,
arms outstretched,
what do you pull
into your heart?

touch

My body needs
the deepest form of
connection.

Within, between.

A reaching out,
a making contact,
as real as skin and bone.
Full of the same
fragile softness.

Is it rare?
Or is it everywhere?

All I know is I am
forever searching for
where the space between
falls away.

us

Your deepest secrets
your darkest shame
the guilt that grasps you
the dream that holds you
the flaws that break you—
this is your human form
at its most human.

This is what makes you
beautiful in my eyes.

And this is how you give me
permission to be human,
too.

close

In the steady press of time
it takes only a
song
scent
smile
touch
taste
to remind me
where I once lived,
and the dreams I held close
for who I have become.

spark

Remind me
to look up
next time we meet,
so I can stop
missing you.

waiting

What did I miss
when I was looking the other way?

All those moments when I was
looking down instead of up,
backwards and forwards,
instead of right here,
tell me,
what did I not see?

I long to know how it feels
for nothing to be too small—
your name, the feeling of
lips and hands and how
the light warms your skin.

The way it feels to breathe
in cold air or taste rain,
or touch paper and pen and
feel my words before dreams
take over and I am lost.

I know, while I wasn't looking,
wrinkles and creases appeared
and the leaves turned and fell,
and children grew into the
people they were meant to be.

I know, while I wasn't looking,
we forgot who we were.

Still the hands keep spinning,
while I try to remember
how to see with my heart.

home

If we get quiet, we will come closer to what makes us feel alive. Pursue and protect what you love with a fierce commitment and never let go; that is the deepest, most powerful expression of yourself. When you are in close connection with what matters most to you, there is nowhere else to be. You are already home.

How do you know you are home?

altar

Tonight
I bow down at the altar
of solitude and silence,
where I find the
mystery and joy of
knowing nothing—
the only God
I have ever felt.

sacred

We all long to be known
for the stories we are,
the feeling that stays with you
after you turn the last page.

Come read my book,
and let me read yours,
cover to cover,
until we hold sacred all that
lives between the lines.

free

I sit here staring
at the empty screen
and the words simply
don't come out.

They litter the floor
of this box
that surrounds me
head to toe
side to side
bottom to top.

Don't get me wrong—
it's a good box
that has served me well.

SALVE: WORDS FOR THE JOURNEY

This box keeps me
smart
trustworthy
successful
compassionate
grateful
for the straight lines and
detour free paths that
allowed me to reach
here.

And yet,
a good box
is still a box,
and the words that have fallen
into these corners and crevices
were the words that could never be said
for being too angry
too loud
too imperfect
too much.

They were words that
would have meant busting out
of cardboard cages
and taking up too much space
in a world that would prefer
a me that was smaller
and more contained.

But now I can't breathe
and the echoes of these screams
seep through the seams,
and it is me,
all of me,
learning that any box
is too small,
any label too narrow.

We are all so much more
than even we know.

wild

To keep my wild heart
beating in this crazy world
is no small feat.

To keep my wild spirit
fighting in this tired body
takes everything I have.

To keep my wild dreams
alive when it's
hard
to
breathe
is all that matters.

body

What my body wanted to tell me
was that it has loved me
since the day I was born.

Perhaps even lifetimes before
and lifetimes after,
in a way that only my cells know.

My body,
an altar for every dream and tear,
a home for my light
to dance and dim exactly
as it needed to through
all the passing days.

My body reminded me of the
miles my feet have walked,
the faces these hands have touched,
the souls these eyes have seen.
The babies that turned
my uterus to womb and
made me a mother.

And finally,
after all these years,
I asked my body back,
"What can I do for you?"

I waited and I listened for
the answer I always knew,
but could never truly live:
"Simply love me in return."

scars

Somewhere between last night's selfie,
and this morning's mirror,
between smudged eyeliner
and traces of old perfume—
there were words.

Somewhere in the clouds
above the morning trail,
heart-opening playlist,
second cup of coffee—
there was a poem.

And the poem was
a deeply familiar desire
for all the mirrors to disappear,
just for today,
to see what would happen—
if I stopped noticing the
scars on my abdomen and groin,
or the silvery lines under my arms,
or the way a round belly settles
and how new wrinkles always tell
the truth of my body.

What if instead we could be
each other's mirrors and reflect
how you made me laugh,
or how I loved our talk,
or how we sat in the car
and sang so loud?

What if I noticed how very gentle
your eyes are, or how it felt
that night to trace the line of your
clavicle from sternum to shoulder?

These are the songs that the
mirror on my wall can't sing.
Not yet, not today.

So down it comes,
off the wall,
replaced by you and me,
and the light only
we can see.

human

In this busy life, we often get distracted by our day to day, or feel pressured to share the airbrushed version of ourselves. And yet we feel most alive and connected when we allow our hearts to speak and listen closely and with care. We can remind ourselves and each other that we don't need to be perfect, smart, beautiful, or accomplished to be worthy of love and time. We simply need to be human, together.

Write about a time when you allowed yourself to be human.

enough

Today,
silence was enough,
settling around me
like the arms
of a lover.

light

Look toward the light
and tell me what you see.

Your angels dancing,
your heart reflecting,
your tears drying.

Let the light remind you,
you are loved.

purpose

For today, I am saying
no. No.
No thank you.

I don't want to be
better.
No self-improvement
wanted.

This drive to
achieve is building,
the self-critical voices
are strong.

So many urges to do
Something.
Anything.

Instead, I sit.

My own disapproval
projected onto the eyes
of the productive,
scurrying,
getting Life done,
climbing the ladder.

Oh well.

For now,
my only purpose is to
Be.

The rest can wait.

signals

I understand how
life feels heavy sometimes,
even when we can't understand
exactly why, even when
we are present, grateful,
kind, blessed.

Sometimes a weight
settles across your shoulders,
a dark and silent shawl
that lingers and hangs.

I don't know the answers
to your particular struggle,
but in case it helps,
here is permission,
for you, for me.

Maybe to sleep in,
or watch the moon watch you.
Maybe kale or chocolate.
Maybe cry or scream
or throw words and blank space
across the pages of your journal.

To slow down or stop,
do less or nothing,
until you can hear
the heart pulsing deep,
the steady rasp of the breath.
the signals of your cells—
they know what you need.

magic

The secret messages
are soft, quiet,
yet full of truth and power,
like the heart itself.

Over and over, they urge me:
Slow
Listen
Touch
Hold
Love
Trust
Laugh
Be.

I long to know the language
of your heart too—
so that, someday soon,
we can understand
each other's magic.

whisper

Holding hands in the dark,
the wash of moonlight spilling
onto the sheets.

A kiss
that lingers long enough
to feel the heat
of muscle and fascia.

The breath of a sunset sky,
the heat of thunder and lightning
pouring cleansing waters from above.

A burgundy leaf,
skidding on the cement.

The light in the hallway,
illuminating words from
heart to pen to paper,
the folded corners and frayed pages
of a faithful book.

Poems that whisper your name
before blooming into song,
footsteps running on gravel.

Where person
meets time
meets place.

Where I meet you.

We are called to wake up—
not just to the immense
joys and catastrophes
but to everything in between.

song

I read my words aloud and for a moment I hear the sound of my own voice. A surprising moment of sensuous beauty, my thoughts into words and pen onto paper and then sung aloud, a soft melody, a new melody that came through me. I have never heard my thoughts come alive in song. It is a sound I want to hear again, turn the volume up, because there is me in rhythm and rhyme, a heart story told.

The words become a path between you and me, through air and so many miles, and I am only grateful for our connection, grateful to hear the echo of my voice in your story too. And then I understand. This is why we write poems, isn't it? These words that cut through all that could matter less, and leave us with simply you and me and this moment that is ours, a private space that only we know. I am so happy we have met here, in this way.

What are the words of your heart-song?

broken

In today's installment of what's beautiful,
I first found what was broken,
until I caught a fleeting glimpse
of what laid beneath.

My son's hair a rat's nest,
but shining through were those
mischievous chocolate eyes.

My daughter sitting on the car seat,
a tired and irritable mess of
not wanting to go to camp, and
crumbs stuck to the back of ripped leggings
because she had saved her cookie
just for me.

Today's hot yoga was a dusty mat
and a space heater in my office,
one down dog and child's pose and savasana.
But I felt the ligaments between my toes
and heard myself exhale
for the first time in days.

I couldn't seem to find the sacred
in this body that feels too heavy
and a mind streaming with anxieties,
until a poem asked me to play.

Yes, this heart aches to stay open
and yes,
there is a miracle
in every filling of the atria,
every systole that pumps life through me,
without my asking or trying
which is a blessing beyond comprehension.

I don't think I will look for beauty anymore
in what is pristine or just so
because I can't live there,
where I don't belong.

Give me what is worn around the edges,
dirty, cracked, tired
so that I can discover gold.

golden

We could wait for a
thousand days and nights,
a lifetime really,
to be given the green light,
the sign that we are good enough
to try, to shine, to be
out there in the world.

Showing up
exactly as we are
without lowering our voices
or keeping ourselves small.

We could wait for eternities
to be perfect enough
for the approval and love of others
while slowly withering inside.

Who are these chosen ones
who can grant the rest of us
permission?

Where do they live in
their golden perfection?

Only you can choose you.

Only you can open the cage door
and allow yourself to peek out,
survey the wide open scene,
and discover the courage that has always
lived in your veins.

courage

In order to speak our truth, we must first own it. In order to own our truth, we must know ourselves deeply and believe that we deserve to hold our own truth to begin with. In the spirit of transparency, this is so very hard for me. I often know my truth through years of therapy, running and writing. All of these bring me into direct contact with my inner world.

But claiming it? Speaking it out loud? Not so easy for me.

It is much easier for me to stay quiet and wish that others will somehow know my needs, wishes, and opinions, than it is to speak up, disappoint, disrupt, or upset. But the funny thing about your truth is...it's a whisper that can't be ignored. It will morph into tears, insomnia, tantrums, cravings.

It will get louder until you sit up and pay attention.

What is the whisper that can't be ignored?

melting

Within us echoes the quiet wail,
"There is no time,
There is no time."

Time is lost in the striving to
fill empty spaces
that can never be whole,
while clocks spin on and on.

If we were to discover time again,
perhaps it would be found in
melting drops of sun into
crimson and orange horizon, or
in the palpable weight of night,
holding orbs of light
in suspended bliss.

Time rests in the leaf fraying at the edges,
and the lush cold of a single snowflake,
lost against the warmth of the tongue.

Time ripples and shimmers through
the water that all of a sudden fills the creek,
and hides in the dry cracked riverbed, too.

Time is the soft hand of my children
slipping away as they walk ahead,
and time is painting dream worlds on canvas
and spinning poems that awaken
the drumming of the heart,
and spark that nameless feeling
deep inside where suddenly
we are not alone.

Who knows where time goes
while we look the other way,
marching to the sound of seconds dropping,
to the echoes of voices wondering
how life disappeared in an instant?

All the while, time waits for us
to discover the eternities
that lie within
this complete second.

spiral

The path is not linear.
I am not racing
from here to there,
towards a finish line
prize for one.

I am not the architect
of a straight line
black and white
life map.

No, the path is a
spiral journey inward,
deep and messy,
full of detours and dead-ends,
vistas and viewpoints,
chaos and despair and
exquisite pain and
heartbreaking beauty.

May I arrive at the end
in one piece,
at peace,
when my time here is
complete.

Hopefully used,
empty,
of all my love,
and full of every drop
of slow honey life
that was offered to this
human form.

spent

What would it be like
to speak the truth
buried deep in the drumbeat
of our hearts?

What would your blood
say to mine?

What would mine
say to yours,
chest to chest,
wrist to wrist?

Today,
I would have told you
everything—
that grief takes over,
that loneliness washes within,
breathing through waves of
shame and silence and lies.

What would happen
if we said it all,
out loud,
absorbing every last
syllable?

Speaking until spent,
speaking until
we become the
freedom of
no more words.

singular

After a million moments
on my knees,
a thousand forks
in the road,
a hundred nights
of stars in the dark,
and infinite
answerless questions—
I remembered
in one singular
breath—
only my heart
knows the way.

away

If we are too busy for ourselves, each other, and what matters most to us, perhaps our lives have led us away from our hearts.

How do you know you have drifted away?

guides

When the only thing I know
is that I am lost,
I search for the truth.

My spirit whispers:

Trust.
Surrender.
Love.

space

Today the sun
took me by the hand
to a place I often
forget to go.

A space deep within
where there is
quiet in noise
stillness in chaos
feeling in thought.

The sun reminded me
that the world inside
is busier and louder
than the world outside.

Until we pause
for just a moment
and then,
pause again—
allowing that space
of silent noticing,
and noticing silence,
to fill the ache of
striving.

reverse

Today was a day of living slow
yet thinking fast, all of which
is to say that life unfolded
only in my head
with little to no direct touching,
or taking it in.

I didn't see the pink bougainvilleas
with their glorious and bright petals,
singing as they drifted to the ground,
pulling me into their gravity.

Until I realized
that one day all of this,
the fallen petals and me, us, these four walls,
my neighbors up the road,
these verdant hills and gravel paths,
these scribbled poems,
these midnight snacks of yoghurt and granola,
all of it would be gone one day.

Who knows when, but gone one day.

Like rain falling in reverse.

Not a trace of what lifts us up and what bleeds,
all so real in this moment,
will remain.

For a second I felt afraid,
insignificant in the heart,
until I felt my spirit stretch.

safe

Today
let's allow ourselves
to be known
for all of who we are.

The raw bruises that hurt
to be touched.
The dark corners that long
to see light.
The sharp edges that cry
to be softened.

We all long to be allowed,
to be held and seen,
even when, especially when,
we turn away from ourselves.

Let us be safe spaces
where we fall into each other,
landing in the open arms
of always being enough.

found

If I pause in quiet suspension

If I drop into profound silence

I discover a moment so soft
that I can feel breath
breathing itself.

opening

Did you hear once
like I did,
that loving was easy?

I want you to know that
my truth is different.

To me, love that matters is
messy.

Like eyes closed,
flinging paint,
writing a poem whose
words won't sing together.

Erasing and creating
this painful art,
retreating and trying again
to discover threads
of beauty in chaos.

Sometimes love
hardens my heart,
and sometimes
there is an opening,
an inhale,
and I feel myself
come to life.

Now I know—
loving means
we don't get to choose
which parts to keep.

love

May love be the intention that carries every breath, every word, every action.

What is your deepest intention?

falling 1

The sky whispered to me tonight
that I no longer have to be afraid
of the sound of heartbreak
or the silence of tears falling
or even the vast expanse of joy
which feels like a first breath
that you can't quite remember.

The sky promised that it would
hold me through all of it,
the way a mother holds a child.
Soft, strong, fierce and ever present,
even when invisible.

So let yourself go,
sang the clouds,
a secret melody for me.
Let yourself fall, fall, fall
and know I will always
catch you.

falling 2

So she chose to trust
the soft song of the sky.

She reached her arms up,
every finger outstretched,
both palms wide open,
tipped her head backwards and
fell, fell, fell.

While waiting to be caught,
she discovered wings she
had never known in this life.

Ready to receive,
ready to fly,
she soared and dipped,
believed and feared.

She remembered,
this is what it felt like
to let go.

To give up her ground
with complete and wild abandon,
until the world became still and
noticed her opening.

In that most quiet moment,
she heard the sky song again—
only now,
recognizing the unmistakable
sound of her own song,
catching her with its
faithful echo.

mystery

New beginnings fall like a
million orbs of snow
onto my outstretched palm.

A single flake,
water and sky meeting
heat and skin.

The beauty is in the mystery,
in the sparks of light glowing
in the black of night knowing,
and in the questions
asking to be lived.

For if we knew how it all ended,
where would we find wonder?

blessings

Saturday morning
phone rings too early
kids' technology beeping
arguments over
what's for breakfast.

Dogs barking and scratching
and dishes in the sink.
A moment of irritation,
skin stretched too thin,
a feeling that bubbles
in my arteries.

I remind myself to
stop, and breathe—
and notice how the
early light floats through
windows and glows.

This stuff of real life
is somehow hard
and gratitude doesn't
come easy.

Yet the light reminds me,
these are the blessings
of the day.

contradictions

Maybe one of the best gifts she could give herself was to allow herself to be all of who she was—without having to choose, without having to defend, without having to explain. Perhaps one of these days, she would grant herself permission to live a story that was full and round and didn't have to make sense to anyone including her.

Tell me about your contradictions.

ordinary

Now is the routine of
wake up and make breakfast
and make lunch and
race kids out the door
and drive to school and
blow hurried kisses and drive
to the same coffee shop where
the same guy who knows my name
makes my iced mocha.

And work and patients
and picking up children
and activities and homework and
no clue what to make for dinner
and reading bedtime stories and
checked-out runs on the treadmill
and scribbling in the margins of journals
and scattered sleepy meditation
and falling into bed before
doing it all again.

Perhaps this daily routine of regular life
is beautiful because it is true,
true in ways that I can touch.

gratitude

Have you ever
known a moment
where it all felt so hard?

Just to put your
feet on the floor,
or get the kids out the door,
or wait at the yellow light,
or walk through the parking lot,
to just notice
one breath and then
the next.

Sky finds you,
and your heart knows:
someone would
give a limb
for your ordinary day.

Pulled we are,
between two currents—
the overwhelm of
daily life and
the wide open space of
gratitude.

We simply
feel all of it,
allowing it all
to be true.

lines

These lines on my face
are the creases and valleys
of love and fear,
heartbreak and joy.

They are the signs
of life fully lived,
and the scars of a heart
trying so hard to
listen.

busy

The trees remind me
that beauty always lives
in the sun and wind and leaves,
even when I am so busy
building a life
that I forget to notice.

nature

I look up towards the open sky and feel part of so much more than myself. I look down at my feet in the dirt and feel grounded. This is how nature holds me.

Tell me about a time nature held you.

water

For you, who grieves tonight,
for you, whose tears fall,
let them fall.

Your tears need no reason,
no explanation of
source or destination.

They are your water,
here because you are here,
living feeling breathing,
taking it in,
letting it out.

They are the cries of
your ancestors and your future,
broken spirits bones hearts,
rising through you and
blessing your eyes.

They are the pain of losing
when we are not ready
to let go or walk away.

So let the tears fall,
let them fall,
into me,
into the rivers,
into the rain.

landscape

The landscape of my body
holds stories that will never be told,
perhaps even words that
I have never known—
ancient stars hidden in
the dictionaries of my genes,
shaping, deleting, evolving
as I move through this life.

My heart holds the raucous crashes
of Indian rickshaws,
and the first caw caw caw
of birds calling at 5 a.m.,
the smell of fresh garlands and tea
amongst the goats and cows roaming
the dusty streets.

This belly holds my grandmother's recipes,
pungent ginger and garlic and golden turmeric
full of love and family and lingering
over empty plates, while
elders wash their gnarled hands
with water poured from silver cups.

This mind carries the wisdom of medicine,
the blood of doctoring,
the thirst to serve beyond myself and
the reach of my two hands.

These feet run miles around the world
like the feet of my father,
blistered, thickened, yet
happy and well worn and used up.

These cells are the DNA
of generations of ancestors,
reaching beyond space and time to
where I cannot see, and yet.

The seeds of my children,
their souls and spirits,
contained in my architecture.

Within lies dust and Earth and broken roads
that somehow led to me, and
onward to the future—
a blessed mystery.

rain

Field notes on mindfulness from a run in the rain: What if you didn't dodge the raindrops like bullets? What if you allowed the rain to become your tears, the wind to become your howl? Allowed the elements to shape your raw edges into soft curves? What if you saw yourself, growing and shifting, in the slippery reflection of the road?

Let your footprints remind you: you have been somewhere, and you are en route to somewhere else. But for this split second, you are grounded in now. Take a breath. Allow the water and wind to whisper towards the warmth rising from you: You are alive.

How do the elements shape you?

path

I am desperate
more times than I care to admit
to know where the path leads.

What will I see and feel
at the end of the road?
Sometimes I imagine
big crowds and standing ovations
and published books and
lives changed.

What actually comes—
bittersweet beauty
in morning coffee,
sticky little hands,
beloved journals
and moments of looking
up at the sky for a reminder
of how good it feels to be small.

Along the way,
bittersweet beauty
comes in tears that fall
from a broken heart and
missed opportunities in
the rear view mirror,
the disappointments of
trying so hard but
losing the game.

Then I remember
the path is just the path
and who knows what is
beginning, middle, end?

undone

I came to the beach to walk
one foot in front of the other,
a slow step by step by step.

I needed to remember all that I forgot.

Feeling my tether come undone
left me groundless and unhinged.
I had forgotten the feeling
of the earth beneath my feet.

A million grains of sand reminded me
of my roots buried deep,
far beyond where my eyes could see.

I was caught in an opaque bubble
filled with the weight of heavy thoughts.

I came to the water to hear
The only thing louder than the sound
of my own voice—
the roar of the ocean, the waves
flooding sand and eroding rock.

I came to see all the people
I had forgotten
when I felt so alone.

I saw endless footprints ahead and behind,
steps of all those who came before and after
on this same journey we enter and exit alone.

I came to walk myself out of stagnation,
to feel the energy of my blood come alive,
my forgotten body move through space.

I came to remember
what it feels like
to live in this world
and not collapse under the weight
of my own paralysis.

In the end,
I was brought to my knees
by sparks of heat and light
playing into infinity.

The universe itself, walking
step by step by step.

energy

I often find myself relating to the moments of my life from a distance—through the filter of my thoughts and judgments. Busy in my head as opposed to settled deep into my breath, body, heart. In this way, lived experiences pass me by in my distraction. But when I slow down enough to drop down and truly enter a moment, I slow the blur, just a little. I become part of the energy that is life. I become the part of life that exists in the details. I am reminding myself again tonight, to drop my filters that only serve to separate.

Tell me about the energy of this moment.

ancient

I read the words of Mark Nepo
underlining and highlighting and
folding every corner of every page.

I copy the lines that belong to me,
fill the pages of my journal,
so desperate am I
to always remember
the words that quiet my thoughts,
and soothe the edges of fear
within my jaw and shoulder.

So desperate am I to never forget
the words that remind me of
seekers seeking,
journey unfolding,
and living the questions
instead of solving the problems.

He writes of ancient poems
that make him feel the same way,
and I wonder if it's all been written before.

If there is nothing new
to be learned or taught
spoken, written, or sung.
where exactly will my words live?

illusion

This is the space between.

The pause of breath holding
not knowing,
uncertainty growing.

The space between
real and illusion,
between dark clouds
pregnant with water, and
rain pouring from skies
in thunderous sweet relief.

Between
dark velvet night and
first shimmery light,
the barely there
naked touch of dawn.

I long to reach across,
forge a bridge
between you and me.

Instead I discover the
weight of air,
there and gone again.

I long for the certainty of
what words come next—
And the final release of
Exhale
Rain
Morning.

Until then,
this space between
is the only space where
we can live our days.

Everything else is simply
dreams and dust.

blank

The page is like the morning
at 5:30 and 6:10 and 6:30.

A canvas I have seen infinite times
and yet never like this,
never this deep shade of violet
unfolding to grey,
tinged with hints of pink and orange
until a proud blue sky emerged.

Until rays of light flooded my room, and
an entire moment within a moment within a moment
was born somewhere
between the weight of sleep
and the open hopeful expanse of
one more new day.

This sun would never rise
in quite the same way, just like
these words that emerged hours later
were somehow hidden like a secret
in the sunrise—
a pleading call to awaken
and pay attention.

questions

What stories visit you in your dreams,
and what do you fear in the 4 a.m. hour,
when you are alone and still and
the light of the moon falls across the sheets?

Who would you be
if self-doubt and worry didn't freeze
the edges of your heart, and if you could only
let the judgment of the crowds fade into nothing?

What songs would you sing while walking
in the rain, head tilted towards the sky
and arms wide open
to catch every cloud falling into you?

What makes your heart ache
and your tears fall and your soul soar,
and what do you hope for with the
fearless spirit of the child you once were?

How do you live the paradoxes
of golden sunrises and city lights,
towering mountains and quiet streams,
that connect you to all that is greater than us?

lifetimes

We are on a late afternoon walk, my 10-year-old daughter and I, on this Wednesday afternoon. School and work are done for the day, and we settle into a brief pause before homework and dinner and the evening routines. We walk towards a gravel path that winds over mossy green hills and creaky wooden bridges. One of our favorite routes to walk. Having rained earlier in the day, clouds intermittently come together and dance apart, shadows arrive and shadows disappear, as the sun travels above us.

Sometimes we hold hands, and sometimes she walks ahead or behind, and dances, twirls, spins. She stops for every single dog, many of them now "regulars" for her. She knows each dog by name and breed and is happy to roll around with them, chat with them, pet them and simply love them. She talks nonstop, chatty and full of dog facts interspersed with the little tidbit stories from the day. She is appalled by the owners who walk briskly by even as she stops to say hello, the ones who are on a mission to get somewhere or are exercising, and aren't able to stop for the dog lovers along the way. Every now and again, she detours off the path to identify the flowers and plants.

She is present, noticing.

Soon, we approach 5:15 p.m. and it is time to turn around and head back home. There is work to be done. I give her a brief warning, letting her know that we will walk for a couple more minutes, perhaps just to that bend up ahead, and then turn back. She shakes her head no, and asks me for just a little more time. "Please? A few more minutes? How about a few more hours? Okay, a few more days?" She turns around and looks at me, waiting to see me laugh at her desire to walk on for days.

And then, one last imploring question, "How about a few more lifetimes, Mama?"

I pause. Yes. A few more lifetimes.

I will take you up on that offer, my love. I would be honored to walk beside you for a few more lifetimes and a few more beyond that if you will have me. I know that sometimes you will walk ahead and sometimes behind. I know that sometimes you will hold my hand, and sometimes you would rather be free. But if you allow me to walk with you for a few more lifetimes, I will gladly be there, always, ready, should you need me. The work of a thousand lifetimes can wait.

We turn around and we walk home. The air has turned a bit brisk, and the wind ripples through the grass and whips our hair around our faces. Shades of deep pink and orange begin to emerge, just as day is tipping to dusk. Our shadows grow long, approaching the same size these days, and soon, her shadow will outgrow mine. The weather turns. The air cools. Cars are rolling home. And the clock ticks on a few seconds more.

I know I must find the grace to balance between this holding on and letting go. I know I must not let her only walk but indeed run free. I know for this moment, I am holding her more than I am surrendering her. And I know we can't hold each other for lifetimes more...but for now, just for now, I will at least hold onto the hope that maybe we can.

Tell me about the balance between holding on and letting go.

meditation

Sitting this morning in meditation.
Eyes closed, breath even.

Okay, cheating maybe just a little
with a cushion behind my back
and another one in my lap,
in the warmth of my bed.

My hand instinctively travels
to rest on my son's back,
soft, warm cloth outlining
the angled wing of his scapula.

Oh, to be young, stretching through skin.

His hand rests on our puppy
who lies next to him, also asleep.

I touch his hair,
unruly, thick, dark, and
feel the rise and fall of
his body, and a
moment of gratitude for
life itself.

The day has not yet begun,
and grey, unfiltered light
peeks around the curtains,
becoming a part of us and this
three-way meditation.

There is a quiet roar that rattles
through the leaves,
a song and dance
that I might not notice again
until night settles many hours later.

And oh, a surprise thought,
I am supposed to be meditating!

Except instead, these words line up
arrange and rearrange,
little tiles clicking and swapping—
no, that's not quite the word
this poem was waiting for.

Again, a light bulb reminder,
I am supposed to be meditating,
as my hand rises and falls
in harmony with my son's accordion lungs,
and his hand rises and falls
in harmony with furry puppy breath.

Then yes,
a knowing arrives in my body.

That this too, this very moment
of stories that want to be told,
and first light amidst howling echoes of wind,
a quiet moment of connected
breath and becoming—
this too is
meditation.

miracle

Sometimes words visit me
in the middle of the night,
flashes of story and song.

I feel like a dreamcatcher,
witness of poems being offered
in ways that I could never have deserved.

The only way to respond is with
profound gratitude,
for these words that chose me of all people.

To be honest,
that is as close to a miracle
as I get these days,
and I will gladly take it.

I will turn on the light and
write what wants to be written,
sacrifice sleep for this feeling
of joy and connection to something
beyond the reach of these arms.

Yes, of course there is the daily work too.
The practice without magic,
the long dry stretches.

But my secret wish is that
they are simply preparation
for these moments of receiving.

Somehow, this midnight grace
reminds me of earlier today,
when hail fell in sudden raucous downpour.

We looked up in surprise and
breathless delight that we were home—
home on Monday morning
that is normally school and work—
to witness this majestic display
of ice falling from the sky.

Finally, finally our chance
to feel something,
to embody something
greater and grander
than we could ever understand.

imperfect

Our imperfection makes us beautiful, and brings us into honest conversation with each other. When we hold ourselves and others to standards of perfection, we struggle to love and be loved.

How do you embrace your imperfection?

grace

If you are anything like me,
next year will be the
Year Of Big Change—
when I finally publish my book,
and lose those last ten pounds,
and organize my closet
once and for all.

Yes, I know,
I too get confused
about how to dream big and
stay present all at once.

So I do the only thing I know to do,
pause
and become quiet,
until I remember that all I really want
is to own the life I have
with grace and courage.

To lead with my imperfect heart,
take the steps my feet
already know to take—
marveling at the uncertain path
that unfolds beneath.

lost

You and I
know the same fear—
the terror of what we
would say and do
if we faced the truth,
asked the nighttime questions.

I wonder what the moon
knows of empty spaces
and lost answers,
and hidden words.

voice

The voice inside only became
small and still
the day you stopped listening.

You couldn't hear your voice, and
what broke you
was how your voice could no longer
hear you.

Instead you heard the loud noise
of outside distraction,
the seductive clamor
of otherworld sounds.

But without the voice within,
there is no compass.

perfect

To all of my people
who feel alone
because of
illness
addiction
loss
or a room full of those
who just don't see you—
know that I see you,
and that you are
Perfect.

Just as you are.

whole

Words, voices. Faces, tears. Bodies, frozen and released. Joy, fear, grief, relief, expressed in shades of sound and silence. All in a day's work. This work of reminding my people—you are already whole—as I am completed, patient by patient, story by story, myself. "It's been quite a journey," one man said today. Yes. It has, hasn't it?

What are the moments that complete you?

fragile

In a different life,
I took scalpel to skin,
cut through fibrous layers of muscle and fascia
to the very deepest core of,
bodies dead and alive.

I have held a heart in my own hand,
felt its indescribable pulsating power.
I have witnessed the first cries
of a baby being born,
and in the next room,
heard the last extinguishing breath,
the final rattle sigh,
as I watched the spirit of death
sweep through the spaces between us.

Majestic and terrifying,
bringing me face to face
with how little we know,
how hard we try,
how fragile we are,
as soft as the riverbed veins
that glow through our translucent paper skin.

Now I save lives in a different sort of way,
wielding the scalpel of deep compassion,
love, actually.
The CPR of Prozac,
breathing life
into dead spirits.

I watch synapses spark and flicker
through hours of witnessing and walking,
together.

All of this, somehow
no more or less important
than the medicine of poetry—
these words that bring life, too.

worthy

"Have I made enough progress? " she asked,
electric anxiety coursing through her words, and
a certain familiar tremble in her voice.

What is the true question, I wondered.
Is she enough now?
Is she worthy now,
of love, of attention, of respect?

Could she finally rest?

Echoes of questions that I have posed to my own mirror,
a visceral knowing that this thirst cannot be quenched
by oceans of water.

A desperate longing to simply be okay,
for no good reason
other than living and breathing.

We all want to believe in our better selves,
she who shimmers in the far-off imagined future.
She who is thinner, smarter, always knows what to say.
She who is popular, stylish, and more mindful of course.

She who is nothing but a mirage, an illusion,
that disappears each time she is touched.

There is no progress.

Only circling back to yourself,
deserving of
all you long for and need.

Take this girl as she is.
Love her fierce.

toast

She told me once that her depression
was a howl with no end.
An aching scream,
moving like restless wind,
rustling the leaves,
leaving the night world uneasy,
and full of a dark distrust.

Why wasn't it okay,
she wanted to know,
to have no clue what she wanted
from this life?
Truth be told,
all she wanted today
was to get out of bed.

Could that be enough?

Because depression—
it makes your stomach heavy,
and your teeth hurt.

Depression colors your retinas grey
and coats the world
with a sickly pallor.

Somehow you don't ever
get to feel the sun and stars,
their brilliance and shine,
as those with clear eyes.

Depression, she says,
is a loneliness
that crawls on hands and knees through
the cobweb corners of your dreams,
and somehow beats you to breakfast,
its shadowed self
buttering toast and slurping coffee.

No one else sees or hears that,
no, they would call you crazy.
They can't feel ten long bony fingers,
how they grip your shoulders so tight that
you can't feel your next breath.

She tells me
that I won't ever understand
what it feels like
to struggle in her skin.

She tells me
that she doesn't expect a miracle,
other than to feel warm-blooded.

I close my eyes
and wish the same for all of us—
that somehow there was a scalpel
or a stethoscope or hell,
even a magic wand
if that's what it took.

How else to ease this inside-out pain
that cannot be seen or held
but is as true
as the words she speaks,
as desperate as all
that will remain unspoken?

She knows
I have no cure.

But she is still here.
I am still here.
Holding on for dear life,
for her,
with her.

release

Shame settles over you, a heavy blanket of black smoke that suffocates you of oxygen, takes hold of your heart beat, kills your life force. Dead inside, hungry for breath.

Take my hand and borrow my grip. Release the truth that has been building inside of you, demanding to be free.

I will always receive you.

Shame cannot live once you speak your words aloud, like a widening sliver of light illuminating a shadowed room.

You will never walk alone again.

What shame are you ready to release?

MONISHA VASA, MD

stain

"The grief comes like acid rain," she said,
looking away as the steady drip-drip-drip
of tears streamed down her cheeks.

It was 7:47 p.m., almost the end of our time.

Night.

The lights of the city blinking on,
shining in through the seventh floor window,
this warmly lit office, holding space
for the both of us to explore
the jagged terrain of pain, of loss.

I felt my own tears, hot,
a clenched fist in my chest,
a sudden loss of control.

Is it okay to cry?
I was crying for her,
but also for all of us,
and for me too.

Yes, for me too.

Which was all I needed to know
as I pushed tears back into the
raw, soft places where they
are born and live and die,
only to pour again one day from torn skies
just like acid rain.

A single teardrop
landed with a soft silence
a dark stain
that wouldn't disappear.

breath

The mind takes us in a thousand restless directions away from here. The breath brings us back, reminding us that here is the only place we can live.

Wherever you are, whatever you're doing, stop and breathe. I'll join you.

becoming

It is late and I am waiting
and I remember the things
my patients said today
were all the things that needed
to be felt and spoken and heard.

Like "I'm so angry" and
in the next breath,
"I think I need to let go of all the hurt."

Yes, me too.

And my patient who can't
remember me anymore,
"Why does nothing feel welcoming?"

I don't know, but I wish it did.

I believe the three of you today
who still feel miserable
but want off the meds,
and I remember how I barely
take my Synthroid.

And one who walked out the door
straight into the arms of your abuser,
and you tell me you can't?, won't? leave.

All I see is your power,
waiting behind you,
waiting for you,
to turn around.

I don't deserve the stories,
these words that shape me into
becoming
more and more me,
these words that merge into
you, me, us.

wish

May your journey
lead you exactly where
you need to go.

May you find home
every step along the way
within your steady whisper.

May you always know
that at the end of the road,
you will return to you—
complete all along.

permission

I realize that we are often afraid to feel, as strange as that may sound. Perhaps we worry that love will end, or heartbreak never will. That our grief will swallow us whole. That the exhilaration of joy is fleeting, or that fear will paralyze us. Yet feeling the sacred spectrum of human emotion, good, bad and everything in between, is what makes us most human.

Allowing our hearts to be cracked wide open—by the breathtaking beauty of a single kiss, or the despair of loneliness—is what keeps our fingers on the fragile pulse of life.

Tell me about giving yourself permission.

scale

Why have I been silent all of these years?

A quiet, sterile surface,
afraid of not having answers,
afraid of my own ignorance and privilege,
afraid of ruffling feathers.

I have been silent.
Silent like tears falling at night,
silent like a flower wilting to powder,
silent like storm clouds brewing.

Silent.

But now, the truth is, I no longer know
the sound of my own truth,
and I can feel the shame of my ancestors' ancestors,
as they wonder how their hearts got
lost in translation somehow.

My silence is a breeding ground
for injustice and fear, a vacuum of sorts
for someone else's words to fill.

No more, no longer.

The weight of my silence has
buried me into the ground.

The weight of my silence has oppressed
more than aggression and hate and prejudice.

The weight of my silence has taken away
freedoms and health and choices and lives
from those who were counting on
people like me to stand up.

No more, no longer.

I will speak.
I will ask.
I will love.
I will write.
I will protect.

Be it a whisper or a roar,
be it a bad poem or a wrong answer.

One word of compassion weighs more
than silence ever will.

alchemy

A life lived in poetry is 10:08 p.m.
on Monday night with my journal and pen
and a restless, racing mind
over tired shoulders that carry the weight
of baggage I can't seem to release.

A life lived in poetry is alchemy,
the transformation of dying into living,
of rumination into red ink,
of ragged breath
into lines and rows that form
on the page.

A life lived in poetry means moments
of playing with words and
bending and breaking rules,
and listening with my whole heart.

My words will never rhyme—
but the foreign is becoming
familiar.

hummingbird

When the grief buries you,
when the anger blinds you,
when you find yourself full
of an emotion with
no name
no color
no volume
no words—
pause, if you can,
and feel the call of
the hummingbird vibrations
of your body, whispering to you.

Reminding you that you
were alive yesterday,
and you are alive today.

Allow the cells to become your
feet that run,
eyes that cry,
voice that screams—
as you and the faceless emotion
become one
pulsing, living, raging being—
until one day, some day,
you can breathe again.

Still here,
Still here,
Still here.

here

This is what living at the edge feels like. This is what the unsettledness of being you and me feels like. This is what it feels like to have stories without margins or endings unravel within. This is what it feels like to live small in the space of the vast night sky and not know where you fit in, if anywhere at all. And yet. You breathe. Nothing changes, nothing comes, nothing goes, nothing feels different. Waves of gratitude don't wash upon you, and positive thoughts don't come flooding in. Lost people don't return and bad endings don't turn good. But there you are, inside all of it, and all of it inside you. For one more minute, finding your ground, sensing your aliveness. After all, still, you are here. You are here.

How do you find your ground?

practice

The mundane dances with the ecstasy.

No way to have one without the other.
No way to have the brilliant sparks of stars
without the haunting shadows of dark.

Without choosing, without preference

We practice being with it all.

MONISHA VASA, MD

shadows

Insomnia,
we meet yet again
somewhere around 4:02 a.m.—
Sunday night, or is it Monday morning?

Scribbling in my journal,
dark eclipsing my words
that I know will make no sense
come morning.

And yet, the words are
desperate to come out, demanding
to be released.

Insomnia, I think,
You should be an official DSM diagnosis.

At 4:02 a.m.,
the shadows of trees stretch across the ceiling,
coil down and wrap themselves around me
like twisted sheets of bark and leaves.
Awake and trapped, as the hollows
in my chest, my stomach, become
jagged
and
sharp.

There is no witness
to loneliness at this hour,
other than the paper and pen
and the quickly fading light of my phone.

At 4:02 a.m.,
my desperate thoughts are like those lottery balls,
frantic
the losing combination always
sucked to the surface.

I start to hear my doctor voice—
fragments of well-intentioned advice
to my polite patients,
nodding in agreement.

Insomnia won't harm you.
Your body will always get the rest it needs.
Everything feels worse at night without distraction.
Oh and no devices before bed.

As the octopus ink of night
slowly lifts to the faintest velvet gray,
when I close my heavy eyes,
I hear the drumming of water.
The metallic ping-ping-ping
against the roof.

Is it real?
Or is it finally a dream?

edge

2 a.m. anxiety,
You are words that don't make sense
stories without endings.
answerless questions
and questionless answers
living and dying all at once.

2 a.m. anxiety
I am dancing with death more than life.
Twirling on a razor's edge if there ever was one,
of when will I look back and
remember this was all a dream,
a fragile glass that falls in slow motion,
shards flying before it even hits the ground.

2 a.m. anxiety,
you are insomnia
oceans of tears
canyons of fears
the sweetness of fleeting kisses
and the aching beauty of near misses.

2 a.m. anxiety,
you are card games and afternoon cups of tea
and talking past midnight on Saturday.
You wrap me in worry of
when will my turn come
and how will I navigate joy and pain
with strength and grace
and what does that even mean?

2 a.m. anxiety,
one day soon,
I promise I will call you by your name.
drain you of power,
loosen your chokehold around my neck
your vice around my stomach—
your what-iffing, future tripping, fear mongering
will dissolve under the light of awareness
that this is all there is.

2 a.m. anxiety,
dim light of a single lamp
until I feel myself here,
breath becoming words and
the weight of this pen in my hand,
ink appearing like mystery,
the sound of silence as night lives on.

2 a.m. anxiety, you are ice,
melting in my chest,
becoming a thousand rivers,
under the heat
of a single heartbeat.

scrolling

Why are there so many reasons
to be lonely on a Thursday night?

Not alone but lonely, and yes,
just a little more lost than usual.

I can't be the only one
who feels this way, although
from the looks of Thursday night
on Instagram and Facebook,
one might think otherwise.

For I am not meditating,
or reading, or writing, or
lifting weights, or coloring, or
drinking on a girls night out,
or even hugging my children,
or doing yoga on the beach, or
remotely changing the world.

No, none of those things.

Instead, I sit for awhile in my towel,
scrolling, thinking about poetry
and regret and staring at
my reflection in the window,
which gave me yet another reason
to feel the stubborn agitation of these
bulges and rolls.

Then comes shame,
and shame again,
at my lack of gratitude,
my wholehearted un-compassion
towards myself, despite everything
I told my patients today and everything
I know to be true about how much worse
life could really be.

But this Thursday night loneliness,
this emptiness that creeps from the
shadowed corners is real.

Not pretty, not social media worthy, but
real in a way that demands to be spoken
and maybe read, heard, received
by someone, somewhere.

How else will we know each other
when we meet?

freedom

I wanted to write a poem but tired seeped from every cell. Four walls surrounded me, and the words wouldn't come, tangled in the silence of their own weight. The residue of the day humid, stuck to my skin, and the voices in my head on auto-loop, a tape recorder without a pause button. But through it all, an observer, the observer, greater than me and my thoughts...reminding me to set down the struggle for just one breath, for there is so much more air out there.

All I want is freedom from myself, which would look a lot like a poem written by my heart, eyes that see a little deeper, a laugh that tilts toward the sky, and control floating away like a thousand bright balloons.

What poem would your heart write in this moment?

unfiltered

Who were you, before you knew
there was someone else you should be?

Who were you, before you devoted
your life to being different
than exactly who you are?

What if you could leave
behind the burden
You thought was you,
and simply be?

Your eyes would shine with the
unfiltered light of
your pure nature,
your honest smile.

Hold on to it—no—
embrace it.
Don't trade yourself in for thoughts
of who you should have been,
while the ground beneath you shakes
with desire to hold you
as you are.

raw

Now and now and now,
be kinder than necessary—

to the stranger who needs
no more than to be seen.

To the child who needs
your late-night voice and
just one more chapter.

To you, your very self, who needs
the strength of your own holding.

Let down the walls that
once seemed to guard and protect
but only divide and keep you
alone.

Listen instead to the truth
echoing in melodic whisper,
the waters running quiet but wise,
alive, in your vessels.

For you always knew,
kindness is the only life force
that will sustain you.

You must heed the voice,
the call of your first raw soul,
before you forget how.

deeper

I exist so often on the distracted surface of life. Take me deeper, into the very tissue beneath. I want to be the expansion and contraction of the alveolus in the lung. I want to be the electric spark between dendrite and axon and the peristalsis of the gut. I don't want to be sweat and skin, never penetrating this body. Help me see the very inside of the womb itself, where I come from. That is the fertile place I remember in the way I walk and hold my head and sleep on my stomach in the night. That is where I will return one day.

What takes you deeper into the body?

profound

Come here, my friend.

Sit with me.

There is nowhere else to be.
There is no one else to be.
There is nothing else to do.

Let's ask the midnight questions,
the ones only you and I know.
from the mundane to the profound,
from birth to death,
and all that lies between.

Pain is pain and not suffering,
when we can live the questions
in each other's reflection.

Pain is pain and not anguish,
when we can be all that we are.
without judgment,
without shame.

infinity

In a single drop of
silence,
we can hear the wisdom song
of our ancestors,
and the cries of our babies
yet to be born.

We can feel
all that is buried
deep within our cells,
if we become quiet enough to
listen.

If we become still enough to
notice all the ways
the breath moves
through the bones
like whispers of wind,
we might know the echoes of
infinity.

woven

The journey towards self-acceptance is proving to be a lifelong practice. It seems more and more that this is the common thread that weaves through so many of my conversations with my patients, friends, and family.

How do we step into the space that only we can occupy?

How do we own our special kind of beauty, one that is woven from our imperfections, flaws, gifts, strengths, and experiences? How do we find the words that capture our power, while holding space for the other? How do we express our deepest longings and fears and wishes, allowing our most vulnerable shadows to emerge? How do we finally do the thing we have always wished to do—the thing we dream about in the dark—even if it makes no sense? How do we trust ourselves, that we know how to make the choices that are best for us, keeping the external and internal critics and naysayers at bay?

The answer to all these questions? I don't know. I haven't figured it out yet. You may not know either, and that is okay. We set the intention that we are worthy of our own unconditional self love. We learn as we grow and fail and learn and listen and try in every moment.

Being gentle with ourselves, and each other, as we start again.

Tell me all the ways in which you start again.

*I want to remember that
it was all real,
that we happened,
that we were here,
that we mattered.*

Dr. Monisha Vasa is a general and addiction psychiatrist, writer, mother, and mindfulness practitioner, living and working in Orange County, California. She is also a scholar of narrative medicine, which has deepened her relationship to the tremendous healing power contained within words and stories. Dr. Vasa considers working with patients during times of suffering to be one of the greatest honors of her life. In treating patients, she often wondered about all of the individuals navigating big and small life challenges, who might never step foot into the office of a psychiatrist. She wanted to find a way to reach the people who might find support and encouragement by flipping through a well-worn book they kept on their nightstand or bag, just as she herself had done so many times with her favorite books. This was how *Salve* was conceived.

Dr. Vasa has previously published two children's books focused on mindfulness and compassion; *Salve* is her first book of poetry to be published.

You can learn more about her work and writing at www.monishavasa.com.